THE
WHITE
MOUNTAINS

A Photographic Journey

THE WHITE MOUNTAINS

A Photographic Journey

Photographs by

Robert J. Kozlow

HUNTINGTON GRAPHICS
Burlington, Vermont

Published by Huntington Graphics
168 Battery Street, Burlington, VT 05401
www.huntingtongraphics.com

Design by Andrea Gray

Cover photo: Mt. Carrigain and Carrigain Notch from Zeacliff
Acknowledgments photo: Arethusa Falls, Crawford Notch
Introduction photo: Great Gulf Wilderness from Mt. Washington

Printed in China through Four Colour Imports, Ltd., Louisville, Kentucky

Huntington Graphics, P.O. Box 373, Burlington, VT 05402

LIBRARY OF CONGRESS CATALOGING-IN-PUBLICATION DATA
Kozlow, Robert J.
The White Mountains: A Photographic Journey / images by Robert J. Kozlow;
text by Jared Gange and Steve Smith
ISBN-10: 1-886064-19-9 (cloth)
ISBN-13: 978-1-886064-19-5
1. White Mountains‹Pictorial works. 2. New Hampshire‹Pictorial works.

CONTENTS

Acknowledgments

Many people were instrumental in the creation of this book.

Jared Gange, my publisher and his assistant, Andrea Gray, worked diligently to compile my best images into an artistic format. Jared has also had to put up with my seemingly daily phone calls concerning the progress of this project!

The employees of the Franconia Notch State Park, Mt. Washington State Park, and Mt. Washington Stage Co., deserve special recognition. William and Jayne O' Connor, Mike Pelchat, Bill Roy, Amy Bassett, Howie Weymess, and Dexter Rust have all been very supportive and helpful in getting me to my photo opportunities in a pinch.

I would also like to thank the Mt. Washington Observatory and Dr. Peter Crane, in particular, for their assistance in obtaining the Mt. Washington images.

Special thanks go to all the friends and hiking partners who accompanied me on this photographic journey and appear throughout the book, most notably Brian Chamberlain, Jeremy Wood, and my very dear friend, Shaun Moe.

I am grateful to you, Steve, for your kind words in the Introduction. Steve Smith and his colleague, Mike Dickerman, have always encouraged me to seek the unique lesser-known locations.

Finally, I dedicate this book to my Mom and Dad whose love, patience, and encouragement made this project possible. It has truly been a labor of love on a wonderful series of journeys through "God's Country."

Robert J. Kozlow
Lincoln, New Hampshire

Old Man of the Mountain – Franconia Notch.

Men hang out signs indicative of their respective trades. Shoemakers hang out a gigantic shoe; jewelers, a monster watch; even the dentist hangs out a gold tooth; but up in the Franconia Mountains, God Almighty has hung out a sign to show that in New Fngland, He makes men.

— Daniel Webster

Foreword

Few photographers have captured the beauty of the White Mountains like Bob Kozlow, and a collection of his work under one cover is long overdue.

At last count Bob's photos had graced the covers of nearly a dozen guidebooks to the region. Many more have appeared in various magazines and other media, including a popular screen-saver. Now he has fulfilled a long-held dream with his own book.

Bob is talented, patient, and a little bit fussy — as a great photographer should be — and the results are stunning. Within these pages you'll find a marvelous assemblage of images, showcasing the peaks, woods and waters of the White Mountain region, in every season.

There are magnificent mountainscapes aplenty, along with the more intimate beauties found in a moss-draped waterfall, a sparkling backcountry pond, or a stand of snow-cloaked softwoods. The area's familiar landmarks are also well represented: covered bridges and village greens, the late and lamented Old Man of the Mountain, the Flume of Franconia Notch, and the storm-beaten crest of Mt. Washington, the monarch of New England mountains.

As an avid outdoorsman himself, Bob is adept at portraying people at play in these mountains. His images inspire you to explore an unfamiliar corner of the mountains, or try out a new recreational pursuit.

Wherever you live, this book will allow you to bring a little piece of the Whites home with you. Even those of us lucky enough to reside here can take delight in Bob's photographic artistry and his passion for the mountains. All who peruse these photos will come away with a greater appreciation for this extraordinary place – and for those who had the foresight to bring its fragile beauty under protection as the White Mountain National Forest and other public lands.

If you can't be in the mountains, let Bob bring the mountains to you. Enjoy!

— Steve Smith

Introduction

As a transplant from southeastern Michigan, I consider my years in New Hampshire to be a blessing and a privilege. Very few photographers have the good fortune to live, work and play in an area that presents limitless photo opportunities. This book is a labor of love that started over fifteen years ago and has only grown stronger with time.

I distinctly remember my first trip to the Flume in Franconia Notch State Park with my parents on a summer vacation. Coming from Detroit, the Flume represented "Shangri-La" to me — an escape to an enchanted forest with covered bridges and waterfalls. Just as unique were the folks managing the state parks — one could tell from talking with them that the mountains were an inspiration in their lives.

My parents thought I would get over my passion for the White Mountains, but I have been hiking this area year round ever since. I see something new and wonderful each time.

It is best to experience the White Mountains in all four seasons and under different weather conditions. Many of the photos in this book are the result of repeated trips to the same location in order to achieve the desired effect.

A poem by Henry David Thoreau best describes my feelings for New Hampshire:

> I long for wilderness
> Woods where the wood thrush
> forever sings
> Where the hours are early
> morning ones
> and the dew is on the grass
> and the day is forever
> unproven
> A New Hampshire everlasting
> and unfallen

Robert J. Kozlow
February 2007

▷ **Sanguinary Ridge Trail – Dixville Notch.** *The open ledges on Sanguinary Mountain (named for the red tint of its cliffs at sunset) provide magnificent views of the Dixville Notch area. Seen in this view are Lake Gloriette, the Balsams Grand Resort and NH Rt. 26.*

VALLEY VIEWS

Roads which pass through the White Mountains provide ample opportunity to view the full range of the mountain landscape. Steep mountainsides soar high above deep glacial valleys, the forest stretches away for miles from high on the Kancamagus Highway, rivers choked with granite boulders rush downward while peaceful lakes reflect distant mountains. In Franconia Notch, the eye is drawn upward to forbidding cliffs and to barren summits, almost four thousand feet overhead.

Sentinel Pine Covered Bridge – Franconia Notch. *Built in 1939, this bridge rests on the trunk of a huge pine felled by the great hurricane of 1938. It spans the Pemigewasset River just above The Pool, in Franconia Notch State Park.*

Mt. Washington Hotel – Bretton Woods. *The Mt. Washington Hotel, opened in 1902, is situated in spectacular fashion at the base of Mt Washington and the Presidential Range, It is one of only three grand resort hotels still flourishing in the White Mountains.*

The Flume – Franconia Notch. *The Flume is a narrow 800-foot long chasm carved by Flume Brook. A boardwalk runs the length of this natural wonder between 90-foot high granite cliffs.*

Mt. Cube Sugar House – Orford. *The town of Orford, on the southwestern edge of the White Mountains, is a noted center for maple sugaring. Gale and Peter Thompson (son of former New Hampshire Governor Meldrim Thompson) operate this sugarhouse and serve pancake breakfasts at Mt. Cube Farm.*

Lost Pond – Pinkham Notch. *Offering a fine view of the east face of Mt. Washington, Lost Pond is accessible via a short walk from Pinkham Notch.*

Glen Ellis Falls – Pinkham Notch. *A well-engineered stone walkway leads visitors to the base of 70-foot Glen Ellis Falls. It has attracted admirers since the mid-1800s.*

Silver Cascade – Crawford Notch. *This long, graceful cascade spills down the steep side of Mt. Jackson in Crawford Notch. It can be viewed from the side of Rt. 302.*

Little Lake and Mt. Chocorua – Albany. *The view across Chocorua Lake to the rocky spire of Mt. Chocorua is one of the most photographed scenes in New England. This photograph was taken from Little Lake, which adjoins Chocorua Lake.*

Mt. Washington seen from Intervale. *A sea of meadow flowers contrasts with the snow-cloaked cone of Mt. Washington in this view across the broad Saco River valley at Intervale.*

▷ **Upper Ammonoosuc Falls – Bretton Woods.** *Located off the Cog Railway Base Road, this is a popular swimming hole. The cold water of the Ammonoosuc River and whirlpool currents under the falls dictate caution on the part of swimmers.*

Kayaking on the East Branch of the Pemigewasset River – Lincoln. *Kayakers navigate the wild, rocky East Branch of the Pemigewasset River under the famed suspension bridge on the Lincoln Woods Trail. The bridge is the hiker's gateway to the Pemigewasset Wilderness.*

Stark. *This picturesque village is well-known for its covered bridge and Union Church, both built in the 1850s. During World War II, German prisoners of war were brought to a camp here to work in the woods of northern New Hampshire.*

Center Sandwich. *With dozens of historic buildings, seemingly unchanged by time, Center Sandwich offers a nostalgic vision of New England's past. It is located on the southern edge of the White Mountains, near Squam Lake.*

Jefferson Meadows – Jefferson. *The open fields of this traditional summer vacation retreat offer sweeping views of the Northern Presidential Range. Farming is still a way of life here.*

▷ **Northern Presidentials.** *Black-eyed Susans with the Northern Presidentials as a backdrop, as seen from Route 2 in Shelburne.*

FLOWERS

In spring and summer the White Mountains explode with wildflowers, over 250 varieties, in fact! From the splendor of lupines in the lower meadows, to lavender rhodora on rocky ridges, to yellow Pond Lilies and Lady's Slippers, to the naturalized orange Hawkweed and Day Lily, to purple violets and Wild Geraniums, to white Snowy Trilliums, Indian Pipes and Queen Anne's Lace, to Pink Lady Slippers, Sweet William and Corn Poppies, there is much to enjoy.

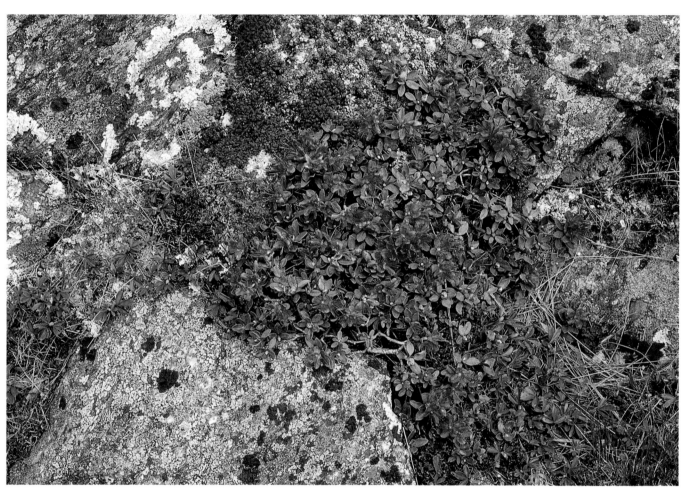

Lapland Rosebay – Mt. Washington. *Found only high in the mountains, in the alpine zone, these beautiful magenta flowers are up to one inch in diameter. This low-lying shrub is a member of the rhododendron family.*

Appalachian Mountain Club's Highland Center – Crawford Notch. *A display of daisies in front of the Highland Center, an educational and outdoor recreation facility. The flower takes its name from ancient English for "day's eye," referring to the yellow sun-like disk in the center.*

Alpine Flowers on Monroe Flats – Mt. Monroe. *The compact cushions and white flowers of diapensia are often found in the most exposed, wind-scoured areas of the alpine zone. This is one of the earliest plants to bloom above treeline.*

Dwarf Cinquefoil – Mt. Washington. *This is one of the rarest plants in New England. In New Hampshire it is found in small numbers only near the summit of Mt. Washington and on Franconia Ridge. It is a relative of the more common three-toothed Cinquefoil, which has white flowers.*

Pink Ladyslippers – Franconia Notch. *This favorite flower is a member of the orchid family. It can be found on many valley trails in late spring/early summer.*

Sugar Hill. *Colorful meadows and the towering mountains around Franconia Notch make Sugar Hill one of the most scenic villages in the White Mountains.*

Daisies – Cannon Mountain, Franconia Notch. *Colorful wildflowers grow in abundance along the roadside during June and July.*

▷ Field of Lupines – Randolph. *These purple to pinkish-white flowers are seen in fields, meadows and along highways in the White Mountains in early June. The Northern Presidentials provide a backdrop for this stunning floral display in Randolph.*

▷ **Zealand Pond.** *This idyllic spot is about a 2.5-mile hike from the car, a little below Zealand Falls Hut.*

Lakes and Ponds

Whether you make the climb up to Lakes of the
Clouds, almost a mile above sea level on the shoulder
of Mt. Washington, cast for trout in Franconia Notch's
Profile Lake or watch a moose wading and grazing in
a shallow mountain tarn, the ponds and lakes of these
mountains are sure to delight. They catch the colors of
sunrises and sunsets and reflect the blazing colors of
autumn, but in winter, the cold and snow reduce them
to fields of white.

Unknown Pond. *This serene and secluded pond rests on a high plateau in the Kilkenny region of the northern White Mountains. The shapely peak of The Horn overlooks the pond; its birch forests turn gold in late September.*

▷ Spaulding Lake – Great Gulf Wilderness. *This small pond lies deep within the Great Gulf, a huge glacial valley encircled by the Northeast's highest peaks. Visiting the pond requires a rugged 13-mile round trip hike on the Great Gulf Trail.*

Upper Carter Lake – Carter Notch. *The rocky cleft of Carter Notch, between Wildcat Mountain and Carter Dome, forms a magnificent setting for this mountain tarn. It is accessible by a 3.8-mile hike on the Nineteen Mile Brook Trail.*

Cherry Pond – Whitefield. *Now part of the Pondicherry National Wildlife Refuge, this 90-acre pond is known for its abundant bird life, unusual bog vegetation, and sweeping mountain views. In this view, Cherry Mountain and Owl's Head are on the right and the Presidential Range is in the distance on the left.*

Lonesome Lake – Franconia Notch. *A lone hiker greets the quiet early morning rays at this sometimes not-so-lonesome mountain pond.*

▷ Cherry Pond – Whitefield. *Easy trails lead to the shore of Cherry Pond, where the Presidential Range sprawls across the horizon.*

▷ **Sandwich Range Wilderness.** *A lovely cascading waterfall along the Fletcher's Cascade Trail in Waterville Valley.*

WATERFALLS

The waterfalls of the White Mountains are justly
famous. While neither terribly high nor powerful,
their number and variety amazes us. They are most
impressive after a good rain or during spring runoff.
Here water plunges into a deep pool, there a cascade
streams down a bare rock face for two hundred feet.
It winds around mossy boulders, bounces down cliff
steps or cuts deeply into a narrow rocky ravine on a
steep, forested slope.

Smarts Brook Trail – Waterville Valley. *This cascade is about a mile up the Smarts Brook Trail in Waterville Valley, an easy walk from Rt. 49.*

Sabbaday Falls – Kancamagus Highway. *Popular Sabbaday Falls can be viewed after a short walk from the Kancamagus Highway. Walkways provide dramatic views from several different angles.*

Arethusa Falls – Crawford Notch. *At 176 feet, Arethusa Falls is the highest waterfall in New Hampshire. It is an impressive sight after a rainstorm. The 1.5-mile trail into the falls provides a pleasant hike over moderate terrain.*

Nancy Cascades – Crawford Notch. *Flowing down from high-country Nancy Pond, Nancy Brook plunges some 400 feet in a series of ledgy drops known as the Nancy Cascades. These spectacular waterfalls can be reached with a 2.4-mile hike on the Nancy Pond Trail.*

The Basin – Franconia Notch. *Thousands of years of churning and scouring action by waterborne rocks and sediment formed this 30-foot wide glacial pothole in the riverbed of the Pemigewasset.*

▷ **Mossy Fall – Randolph.** *Hikers climbing Mt. Adams are rewarded by this emerald-fringed gem of a waterfall just as they are about to enter King Ravine.*

▷ **Zeacliff Outlook.** *This rocky perch on Zealand Ridge overlooks Mt. Carrigain, Carrigain Notch and the eastern Pemigewasset Wilderness and is noted as one of the finest viewpoints in the White Mountains. It is accessible from near Crawford Notch via the Zealand Trail and Twinway.*

ON THE TRAIL

The White Mountains are a hiker's dream. A well-maintained and extensive network of trails crisscross the region. The novice as well as the expert hiker have breathtaking vistas available to them from Mt. Washington to Mt. Moosilauke. The Presidential Range offers very challenging hikes and climbs. While summer and fall are the most popular seasons for hiking, hardier souls will thrill to seasonal changes and spectacular winter scenes.

Great Gulf Trail. *This trail follows the West Branch of the Peabody River through the long glacial valley known as the Great Gulf. It climbs up the steep headwall and ends at the Gulfside Trail just below the summit of Mt. Washington. It is a rugged and spectacular route in any season.*

Lakes of the Clouds Hut. *At an elevation over 5000 feet, the Lakes of the Clouds Hut is the highest in the Appalachian Mountain Club's chain of mountain hostelries. It is set in a windswept saddle between Mt. Washington and Mt. Monroe.*

Caps Ridge Trail – Mt. Jefferson. *Starting at the high point on Jefferson Notch Road, the Caps Ridge Trail provides a rocky and rugged route to the summit of Mt. Jefferson in the Northern Presidentials.*

Franconia Ridge Trail – Mt. Lincoln. *The open crest of Franconia Ridge is one of the most spectacular hiking routes in the East. This view from Mt. Lincoln looks across the Pemigewasset Wilderness to Owl's Head Mountain and Mt. Carrigain.*

Southern Presidentials from Mt. Washington. *An Appalachian Trail "thru-hiker" pauses to admire the Southern Presidentials from the summit of Mt. Washington.*

▷ **Giant Stairs from Mt. Crawford.** *The unique formation known as the Giant Stairs is on Montalban Ridge in the Presidential Range-Dry River Wilderness. This view is from the rocky summit of Mt. Crawford, which is reached via a spur trail off the historic Davis Path.*

Welch Mountain – Waterville Valley. *This huge granite slab is one of several ledge sections along the scenic Welch-Dickey Loop Trail. This 4.5-mile trail provides a "big bang for the buck" with many open views at a relatively low elevation.*

◁ Sanders Bridge – Randolph Path. *Spanning Cold Brook along the Randolph Path on the northern slopes of the Northern Presidentials, this bridge was built in 1976 as a memorial to Miriam Sanders, a longtime active officer and member of the Randolph Mountain Club.*

Upper Greeley Pond – Mad River Notch. *Sequestered in the deep cleft of Mad River Notch, Upper and Lower Greeley Ponds lie between the steep sides of Mt. Kancamagus and Mt. Osceola's East Peak.*

Signal Ridge Trail – Mt. Carrigain. *A hiker pauses on the open crest of Signal Ridge to take in the view towards Mt. Washington and slide-scarred Mt. Lowell.*

Rumney. *Located near Plymouth, the Rumney climbing area attracts sport climbers from all over the country.*

Tuckerman Ravine – Mt. Washington. *A lone hiker peers into Tuckerman Ravine from the Lion Head Trail.*

Bondcliff Trail – Pemigewasset Wilderness. *Franconia Ridge and Mt. Garfield provide the backdrop for this photo of young hikers on an adventurous 19-mile day trip to spectacular Bondcliff.*

Star Lake – Mt. Madison. *This shallow, rocky tarn is set in the high, craggy col between Mt. Adams and Mt. Madison. It was named by 19th century author Moses Sweetser "because it mirrors so perfectly the constellations above."*

Great Gulf Wilderness from Mt. Washington. *A sea of green and gold highlights this fall foliage shot with the huge glacial cirque of the Great Gulf as a backdrop.*

▷ Hermit Lake – Mt. Washington. *Hermit Lake lies at the base of Tuckerman Ravine, and the ravine's steep headwall can be seen in the distance. Nearby lean-to shelters are used by hikers and spring skiers.*

Mt. Washington. *Winter climbers take in the view from the top of the Tuckerman Ravine Trail near the summit of Mt. Washington.*

Mt. Moosilauke – South Peak. *Massive Mt. Moosilauke, anchoring the southwestern corner of the White Mountains, has long been a hiker's favorite. A traverse from the South Peak to the main summit reveals magnificent views in all directions.*

Signal Ridge Trail – Mt. Carrigain. *The main summit mass of Mt. Carrigain looms ahead in this view from Signal Ridge. An observation platform on the summit provides one of the finest panoramic views in the White Mountains.*

Gem Pool – Ammonoosuc Ravine Trail. *This idyllic spot is found on the Ammonoosuc Ravine Trail, 2.1 miles from the parking area. It is a good spot to rest because from here on, the trail is much steeper.*

Madison Spring Hut – Mt. Madison. *Built in 1888 near the col between Mt. Madison and Mt. Adams, this was the first of the AMC's high country huts. The present hut was rebuilt after a fire in 1940 and accommodates 50 guests. It is open from early June through mid-September.*

Mt. Washington Cog Railway. *Opened in 1869, this was the first mountain-climbing cog railway in the world. A unique cogwheel system provides both traction and braking. The average grade along the 3.25-mile track is 25%, increasing to 37.5% at the Jacob's Ladder trestle.*

Lakes of the Clouds Hut – Dry River Trail. *Hikers approach Lakes of the Clouds Hut on the Dry River Trail. The hut is usually reached by either the Crawford Path or by the three-mile Ammonoosuc Ravine Trail, which originates near the base of the Mt. Washington Cog Railway.*

▷ **Arethusa Falls – Crawford Notch.** *A hiker enjoys the view and cooling spray at the foot of Arethusa Falls, the state's highest.*

▷ **Mt. Willard – Crawford Notch.** *Renowned for its magnificent view of Crawford Notch, Mt. Willard's summit is relatively easy to reach. It is a favorite among beginning hikers.*

SUMMITS

The White Mountains have 48 summits over 4,000'
with one of them—Mt. Washington—registering 6,288',
making it easily the highest in the Northeast. Five others
are over 5,000'. The higher peaks reach well above treeline, providing the visitor with a fascinating transition
from a temperate forest zone to the windswept reality
of a sub-arctic environment. Tree growth ends abruptly
and only lichens, grasses, sedges and a few species of
wildflowers can survive on these rocky heights.

Franconia Ridge. *The Franconia Range offers the second highest ridge in the White Mountains. The walk along the open crest on the Franconia Ridge Trail is as spectacular as any in the East.*

▷ **Mt. Garfield – Pemigewasset Wilderness.** *The bare rock summit of this 4500-foot peak provides a striking view over the Pemigewasset Wilderness and surrounding mountain ranges.*

Mt. Washington. *In the clouds: the view from the summit of Mt. Washington of the parking lot at the top of the Mt. Washington Auto Road.*

◁ Bondcliff – Pemigewasset Wilderness. *Nine miles by trail from the nearest road, this 4265-foot peak commands sweeping views over many valleys and ridges with virtually no visible signs of civilization.*

South Twin Mountain. *Panoramic views are the hiker's reward from this high, open peak in the Twin Range. A popular ascent route is via the Gale River Trail, Garfield Ridge Trail and Twinway, passing Galehead Hut en route.*

▷ **Mt. Chocorua – Albany.** *This rocky pinnacle at the east end of the Sandwich Range is immensely popular with both hikers and photographers. Countless peaks can be seen from its summit; looking north one sees Mt. Eisenhower, Mt. Monroe, and Mt. Washington.*

Mt. Liberty – Franconia Notch. *This 4459-foot peak on Franconia Ridge provides outstanding views east into the Pemigewasset Wilderness, north along Franconia Ridge, as seen here, and west over to Cannon Mountain and the Kinsman twins.*

Mt. Pierce – Presidential Range. *Rock cairns blazed in white guide hikers along a section of the Appalachian Trail on Mt. Pierce in the Southern Presidentials.*

▷ **Mt. Osceola – Kancamagus Highway.** *This ridge looms impressively on the south side of the Kancamagus Highway just east of the town of Lincoln and Loon Mountain Ski Area.*

FALL

For many, fall is *the* time to visit the White Mountains. Starting in mid September and running for about a month, fall foliage is a complex event. It starts in the north and moves south and at higher elevations and moves downhill. Different species each have their own timetable. The yellow poplar, birch and elms start off, followed by the flaming red and orange sugar maples, and finally the brown oaks and beeches conclude the color symphony.

Mt. Chocorua – Chocorua Lake. *Rising beside Rt. 16 in Tamworth, 3500-foot Mt. Chocorua is a beautiful sight in any season and boasts many fine hiking trails. At its base Chocorua Lake provides ample boating and fishing opportunities.*

Late fall/early winter – Franconia Notch. *The gold and orange of the valleys give way to the early snows of the higher elevations.*

Mt. Washington from Mt. Eisenhower Wayside Park. *The often-overlooked Wayside Park is situated along Rt. 302 south of Bretton Woods. It offers a gorgeous view of the Presidential Range along with a steep hill that is excellent for family sledding in the winter.*

Lower Falls – Kancamagus Highway. *Fall foliage highlights this very popular Swift River swimming hole on the eastern end of the Kancamagus Highway.*

Wentworth. *This classic New England village, with a triangular town common, is set in the Baker River valley in the southwest-ern corner of the White Mountains.*

Squam Lake from Doublehead Mountain. *Ledges on Doublehead and other peaks in the Squam Range afford views of the complex shoreline of Squam Lake. Squam Lake was the setting for the movie On Golden Pond.*

Pumpkin people – Jackson. *Every year in Jackson during the foliage season, businesses and private homes alike celebrate the return of the pumpkin people with a community pumpkin-decorating competition.*

▷ **St. Matthews Episcopal Church – Sugar Hill.** *Set on a high ridge with views to Mt. Lafayette and Cannon Mountain, this church and the surrounding homes and farms make up one of the state's prettiest communities.*

Tamworth. *Tamworth village is a compact crossroads community boasting a Victorian inn, the Barnstormers Summer Playhouse and the Remick Country Doctor Museum.*

▷ View from Owl's Head – Cherry Mountain. *This magnificent view is obtained from the rocky ledges of Owl's Head, a spur of Cherry Mountain. It can be accessed from Rt. 115 by the Owl's Head Trail or by a longer route via the Cherry Mountain Trail and Martha's Mile.*

Birches – Shelburne. *The famous birches of Shelburne are found along Rt. 2 east of Gorham.*

◁ East Branch of the Pemigewasset River – Lincoln. *This view across the East Branch was obtained from Hancock Campground on Rt. 112. The Pemigewasset River has many favorite swimming holes and is popular with local anglers.*

Cherry Mountain from Cherry Pond. *The Pondicherry National Wildlife Refuge features several thousand acres of forest, marsh and bog, along with Cherry Pond and Little Cherry Pond.*

▷ **Twin Mountain.** *A small pond shows off its brilliant fall foliage colors.*

▷ **Cannon Mountain summit.** *As the sun gets ready to set it casts a vibrant pink hue on the snow-capped Franconia Ridge, including Mt. Lafayette, Mt. Lincoln and Little Haystack.*

WINTER

In the winter these mountains are transformed. The barren summits and ridges, now white with snow and ice, stand out sharply against the sky. Streams and waterfalls become a mix of frozen and fluid grace and the dense evergreen forests are encased in ice. Ponds hibernate until spring. But there is plenty of human activity. Skiers, snowmobilers and ice climbers are in their element. And even in winter hikers tramp up and down the mountain trails, relying on their trusty snowshoes.

Mt. Tecumseh – Waterville Valley. *Waterville Valley is one of the most popular ski areas in New Hampshire, with dozens of ski trails lining the face of Mt. Tecumseh.*

Cannon Mountain summit. *The unique condition called an "undercast" occurs when the mountaintops appear as islands in a sea of clouds. This particular view features Mt. Liberty and Mt. Osceola.*

Echo Lake – Franconia Notch. *Surreal scenes such as this can sometimes be experienced in late October and early November, before ice forms on the lakes of Franconia Notch.*

The Pool, Pemigewasset River – Franconia Notch. *The Pool is an unusual, 100-foot wide pothole in the Pemigewasset River, hemmed in by high cliffs. This view is taken from the Sentinel Pine Covered Bridge.*

Randolph. *A pastoral early morning view showcases the Presidential Range in the background.*

Cannon Mountain – Franconia Notch. *Undaunted by frigid February temperatures, a skier descends Vista Way. Mt. Lafayette and the Franconia Range are in the distance.*

Great Gulf Wilderness. *The Great Gulf Wilderness shows off its winter garb in this shot taken along the Gulfside Trail on Mt. Washington. From left to right, Mt. Jefferson, Mt. Adams and Mt. Madison.*

Tuckerman Ravine. *The view from the Hermit Lake area at the base of Mt. Washington's famed Tuckerman Ravine. The ravine's Headwall and Little Headwall are clearly visible.*

Old Man of the Mountain – Franconia Notch. *The Old Man peers over a wintry scene in Franconia Notch. Sadly, this New Hampshire icon fell in May 2003, a victim of the relentless forces of nature.*

◁ Scar Ridge from an outlook on the Kancamagus Highway. *Beautiful winter scenes such as this one overlooking rugged Scar Ridge can be found by exploring the Kancamagus Highway during the winter months.*

▷ **Mt. Washington from Wildcat Mountain.** *The classic view of the east side of Mt. Washington with Tuckerman Ravine on the left and Huntington Ravine on the right.*

MT. WASHINGTON IN WINTER

In summer, Mt. Washington's summit is a busy place; visitors arrive on foot, by car, by motorcycle and by train. Winter is a different story. The average temperature in January is 10 degrees and the average wind speed is 50 miles per hour. A Sno-Cat plies the now snow-covered auto road, ferrying supplies and visitors to the bunker-like weather observatory on the summit. Visitors venture outside warily, never straying far from the safety of the summit buildings.

Sunrise from Mt. Washington. *It is an unforgettable experience to see the sun rise over Wildcat Mountain on a beautiful winter morning.*

▷ Moonrise – Mt. Washington. *This view of Mt. Washington in winter was taken from the back porch of the historic Mt. Washington Hotel in Bretton Woods.*

Tuckerman Ravine. *Winter hikers trek along the Tuckerman Ravine Trail. The ravine's headwall looms in the distance. From late March into June the headwall of Tuckerman Ravine and nearby chutes attract thousands of skiers and spectators from all over the Northeast.*

◁ **Huntington Ravine.** *One of the great ravines on the east side of Mt. Washington, Huntington is a mecca for ice climbers. Among the obstacles they face are 1500 feet of elevation gain, an exposed alpine setting, windslab conditions and cornices, and potentially extreme weather.*

Mt. Washington summit. *This moonscape shot was taken on an incredibly calm winter morning with the temperature at twenty below zero.*

Mt. Washington summit. *Rime ice encases the old stage office, one of the summit buildings. Rime, which is frozen fog, forms when the summit is enshrouded in clouds with cold temperatures. These formations are created more rapidly with high winds.*

Mt. Washington Observatory Sno-Cat ascending the Mt. Washington Auto Road. *An EduTrip weekend sponsored by the Mt. Washington Observatory offers an unparalleled opportunity to visit the summit of Mt. Washington in winter. Participants ascend to the summit via Sno-Cat; this photo was taken near the 5-mile mark on the Auto Road.*

◁ **Mt. Washington Observatory.** *The summit observatory building is encrusted with rime. The fluted and sculpted snow formations in the foreground attest to the force of the wind.*

Lonesome Lake – Franconia Notch. *Dawn in the White Mountains: the sun rises over the Franconia Range.*